In One Day

IN ONE DAY

BY TOM PARKER

Illustrations by the Author

HOUGHTON MIFFLIN COMPANY BOSTON 1984

To Cally

Library of Congress Cataloging in Publication Data

Parker, Tom.
  In one day.

  1. United States—Social life and customs—1971-
—Miscellanea.   I. Title.
E169.04.P36   1984   031'-02   84-19257
ISBN 0-395-35368-8 (pbk.)

Printed in the United States of America

H 10 9 8 7 6 5 4 3 2 1

It takes about two years for most statistics to surface in published form. The calculations in this book are based on 1982 population estimates. For more information about associations refer to the *Encyclopedia of Associations* published by Gale Research Company, Book Tower, Detroit, Michigan 48226.

Designed by Kat Dalton and Tom Parker

ACKNOWLEDGMENTS

Thanks to Cheryl Russell who helped create this project. Thanks to Caroline Eckstrom for her personal and logistical support. Thanks to Kat Dalton who helped turn a roomful of material into a tightly-knit book on an even tighter schedule. And thanks again to Gerard Van der Leun for his editorial encouragement. Also, thanks to Walter Pitkin, Loretta Heimbuch, Rick Eckstrom, Ann Lloyd, Steve Parker, and the many people who patiently suffered all sorts of indignities while modeling for the illustrations.

Special thanks to American Demographics magazine where much of this material appeared from 1980 to date. Thanks to Bryant Robey who boldly stationed IN ONE DAY on the cover of the magazine, and to Peter Francese for his counsel and support.

And finally, an extra special thanks to my friend Michael Rider for his day-to-day advice. As art director of American Demographics, Mike did the stunning color work reproduced in this book.

INTRODUCTION

In one day the hearts of Americans pump more than 400 billion gallons of blood, equal to the flow of the Mississippi River at Vicksburg.

This book is about the 24-hour rhythm of life in the United States. It is about America as a cultural organism that daily grows by 5,500 people and daily pumps 400 billion gallons of blood through 236 million human hearts. It is about a country that eats 6.5 million gallons of popcorn a day.

IN ONE DAY illustrates the human size of the United States. If all 236 million Americans were squeezed together into one standing-room-only crowd, they would take up 12.7 square miles of floor space. If the United States were the size of this page, every person in the country could stand comfortably on the period at the end of this sentence. That doesn't seem like very many people. But if all 236 million people stood single-file in a line, they would stretch 67,000 miles, or more than 26 times the width of the United States. That seems like a lot of people.

So, just how big is the American crowd? Obviously, big numbers alone are confusing. In this book, I measure Americans by measuring what they do—what they eat, what they buy, what they build, and what they make a mess of.

IN ONE DAY contains 365 separate entries, a fact a day for a year. Some of the entries are accompanied by scale drawings to better show what the numbers mean; I find it easier to visualize a pile of, say, 52 million aspirin than to understand the number by itself. For the most part, I avoided the use of looming perspectives in these illustrations. Towering buildings and fish-eye views would have added impact but lessened accuracy. Strung together, one after another, the numbers draw a picture of Americans that is dramatic enough.

How big is a crowd of 236 million people? Big enough to eat 2,900 tons of chocolate candy every day. Once you know that, it's not so hard to understand why Americans jog 28 million miles a day and use 550,000 pounds of toothpaste.

Where did I get all these figures? Anywhere I could find them. Our society is laced with numbers. There are truckloads of statistical abstracts, market surveys, and corporate reports just waiting for someone—anyone—to shovel through them. Government agencies alone publish more statistics than anyone could hope to read, and the scientific community cranks out 6,000 to 7,000 technical papers every day.

One great source of unusual numbers is private associations. There are literally thousands of them. There is the Hickory Handle Association, the Hotdog and Sausage Council, the Sponge and Chamois Institute, and the American Producers of Italian Type Cheese Association. There's the Caterpillar Club, an association with 16,000 members whose lives have been saved by parachutes. Need some information about name plates? Call the National Association of Name Plate Manufacturers. Vacuum cleaner bags? Give their group a call. No, they probably won't answer, "Vacuum Bag Manufacturer's Association." These people get more than their fair share of crank calls. They are more likely to answer with an ever-so-slightly apologetic, "Association Headquarters" or at best, "VBMA." But call them and you are apt to end up with one of the world's leading authorities on vacuum cleaner bags. If he or she doesn't know how many vacuum cleaner bags Americans buy every day, who does?

In One Day

1. 150 Americans have a nose job, 150 have the bags removed from under their eyes, 100 have a full face lift, and 32 have their ears fixed so they don't stick out so much.

IN ONE DAY:

2.

Some 8,400 Americans celebrate, or try their best to forget, their 40th birthdays.

3.

Nine Americans die by accidentally swallowing or inhaling objects other than food, and at least a dozen children are rushed to hospitals with toys stuck somewhere inside them.

4.

Americans print more than a quarter million dollars of counterfeit money, enough to buy 30,000 copies of this book. The U.S. Secret Service claims that 90 percent of the funny money is seized before it reaches the public.

5.

Americans buy 190,000 wristwatches. More than half are purchased as gifts.

6.

Americans eat 228,000 bushels of onions. That's a pile of onions 120 feet wide and 75 feet high.

7.

Thirty-four million Americans pack more than 2 million bushels of lunch to work in lunch boxes and brown paper bags.

8.

Americans gargle 69,000 gallons of mouthwash. They top that off with a quarter million packs of mints and breath fresheners.

9.

Americans dream up seven or eight new products to sell in supermarkets and drugstores.

10.

25,000 Americans discover they have lice.

entertainment and rec-
reation. That's about as
much as they spend on
national defense.

13.

Americans steal $20,000
from coin-operated
machines.

14.

Americans throw out
200,000 tons of edible
food—about 8 million
cubic feet of chow. The
giant cube in the illus-
tration outlines 8 mil-
lion cubic feet.

15.

Americans toss back
15.7 million gallons of
beer and ale; that's 28
million six-packs. The
bottles and cans from a

IN ONE DAY:

11.

Americans buy 120,000
new radios. This coun-
try currently has 500
million working radio
receivers. If they were
spread evenly across
the United States, in-
cluding Alaska, there

would be one radio for
every five acres of land.
A news addict hiking
cross-country would
never be more than 233
feet from a working
radio.

12.

Americans spend $700
million, or more than
$8,000 each second, on

day's drinking would fill a baseball stadium to a depth of 30 feet.

16.

Americans produce 110,000 tons of salt. That much table salt would fill a salt shaker 214 feet tall and 138 feet in diameter.

17.

4,100 Americans suffer a heart attack, and 1,500 of them die. Heart disease of one kind or another claims 2,700 lives a day.

18.

The average American eats one teaspoon of artificial colors, flavors, and preservatives. That

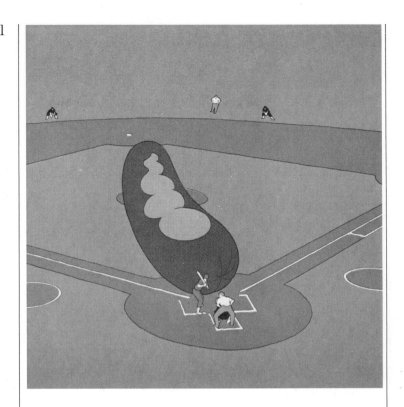

adds up to almost four pounds a year for every person.

19.

Americans eat 47 million hot dogs, the equivalent of a hot dog 30 feet in diameter and half the length of a football field, or roughly 100,000 cubic feet of whatever hot dogs are made of. Baseball fans can imagine a pack of 10 wieners like the one above—14 feet thick and long enough to reach from the pitcher's mound to home plate.

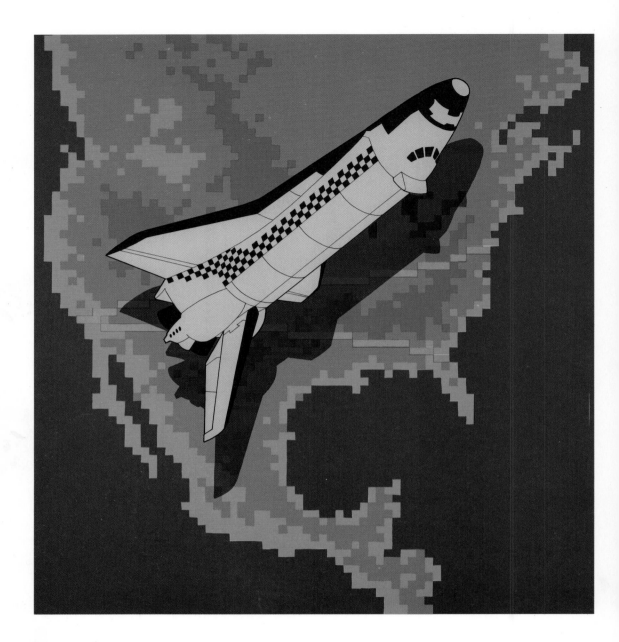

20. Fifteen million Americans are on the road or in the air 100 miles or more from home. That's enough people to form a ticket line that reaches across the United States and back again.

IN ONE DAY:

21.

Airport security personnel screen 1.7 million passengers and visitors for weapons or bombs. They find about six weapons a day.

22.

There are nine or ten accidents involving aircraft of one kind or another. Three or four people are killed, the same number who die in boating accidents.

23.

23,000 Americans head overseas for business or pleasure. According to the most recent figures, Americans collectively see the world on $35 million a day.

24.

American back yards sprout another 1,000 satellite TV dishes. American living rooms sport 17,000 new video cassette recorders.

25.

Americans buy 50,000 new television sets (60 percent of them are color). If you spread them evenly along the road between New York City and Hollywood, they would be just over 300 feet apart—less than a minute's walk. Television addicts could easily walk from one TV to the next during commercials and never miss part of a show.

26.

Americans publish 125 new books. There are 15 new works of fiction, 8 new children's books, 20 books on sociology and economics, and 6 books on history. There are 5 new reference books to refer to, 8 or 9 books on medicine, 9 on philosophy or psychology, 15 on science and technology, and 6 on religion. Americans buy almost 5 million books a day.

alone, more than 20 vehicles a day are simply abandoned. Twenty thousand cars would jam-pack a 55-acre junkyard or form a line of bumper-to-bumper traffic more than 50 miles long.

30.
Vandals do damage to public schools totaling $550,000.

IN ONE DAY:

27.
Americans spend $2.5 million washing their cars.

28.
Americans spend $40 million for automobile repairs and replacements caused by rust. That's enough money every day to buy 2,000 stainless-steel De Loreans at their currently discounted price.

29.
Americans throw out 20,000 passenger cars and 4,000 trucks and buses. In New York City

31.
Americans make half a million car and truck tires. Standing side by side like Lifesavers, they would stretch more than 50 miles. Americans also spend $250,000 a day getting rid of old tires. About 18

percent are retreaded, 3 percent are burned as fuel, and the rest end up in landfills, creeks, or painted white with plants inside them.

32.

Highway potholes cost Americans $100 million in car parts, tires, gasoline, and medical expenses.

33.

Americans driving on unpaved roads stir up 81,000 tons of dust. That's enough to cover a football field—the Dust Bowl—to a depth of 48 feet.

34.

Americans wear more than 3 million pounds of rubber off their tires—enough to make a quarter million new tires.

35.

Three hundred inventors take their inventions to the U.S. Patent Office; 180 of them are granted a patent. Fewer than 3 of them ever make any money from their invention.

36.

Americans spend $200,000 to buy roller skates. About 300 people a day skate their way into a hospital emergency room or doctor's office.

37. Americans produce 33 million pounds of aluminum, enough to make 132 square miles of aluminum foil. That much foil could wrap two dozen spuds like the whopper shown here—the Big Potato. And every day, Americans recycle 78 million aluminum cans. That's enough to make 18 Boeing 747 jetliners.

IN ONE DAY:

38.

Public sewers in this country drain off enough organic waste to make 3,000 tons of nitrogen plant food. That's equal to 54 million pounds of commercial fertilizer.

39.

Americans collectively filter 10 billion gallons of liquid with their kidneys, enough to fill half a million kidney-shaped back-yard swimming pools.

40.

Americans use 450 billion gallons of water for their homes, factories, and farms. That's enough to cover Manhattan to a depth of 96 feet.

41.

Seven or eight Americans seriously burn themselves with hot tap water.

42.

About 4,200 billion gallons of water fall on the lower 48 states. That's enough rain to flood Manhattan, 22.2 square miles, with 900 feet of water.

43.

American drivers use 313 million gallons of fuel—enough to drain 26 tractor-trailer tank trucks every minute. If this country ran out of gas, it would need an emergency gas can 400 feet wide and 332 feet high to get it through the day.

44.

The United States government spends more than $2 billion. Federal computers dole out $5.5 million of it without any human supervision.

45.

Americans sell 750 tons of cauliflower. The whopping head of cauliflower in the drawing weighs 750 tons.

are for drunkenness, driving under the influence, or violation of some other liquor law.

49.

More than 20 convicts escape from state and federal prisons. Like the escapees, facts on the number recaptured are hard to find.

50.

Three thousand Americans are confronted by a robber. Five hundred of them discover that the robber is someone they know.

IN ONE DAY:

46.

One hundred robbers find it convenient to rob a convenience store.

47.

Full-time prisoners in this country—there are 500,000 of them—eat more than a million pounds of food. That's enough groceries to stuff 25 tractor-trailer trucks.

48.

The police in this country arrest the equivalent of 500 busloads of people—28,000 in all. One-quarter of the arrests

51.

The Armed Forces are looking for a few good men—60 of them desert and almost 200 go AWOL. The U.S. Marine Corps has the highest rate of desertion and AWOL; the U.S. Air Force has, by far, the lowest.

52.

Sixty prisoners are released before their sentences are up because their jails are too crowded to hold them.

53.

408 Americans officially join the ranks of missing persons. Happily, 391 are officially found each day—a net loss of only 17. Unofficially, as many as 5,000 children disappear every day. Most of them, though no one knows how many, run away on their own; 275 are snatched by estranged parents. Fifteen or 20 are picked up by strangers and never heard from again.

54.

One thousand Americans have their pockets picked and 375 have their purses snatched. The pickers and snatchers make about $250 per pick and snatch.

55.

Thirteen or fourteen human bodies turn up that can't be identified.

56. More than 40 American teenagers give birth to their third child. Six women age 40 or older have their first baby. Eighteen children are born to fathers who are older than 55.

IN ONE DAY:

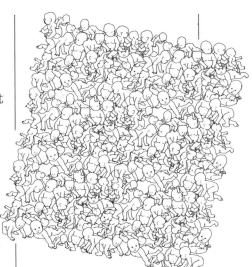

57.

Almost 6,000 teenagers have sexual intercourse for the first time.

58.

Americans spend more than $10 million on pornography. At least a quarter million people a day attend full-length adult movies.

59.

Sixty-eight teenagers are arrested on charges of fraud or embezzlement and 78 children under the age of 16 are arrested for stealing a motor vehicle. On the other hand, 70 senior citizens are picked up for disorderly conduct—the single largest category of arrests for people age 65 or over.

60.

Fifteen hundred Americans are physically attacked by a friend or relative.

61.

4,250 Americans have an abortion.

62.

Five Americans have their citizenship revoked.

63.

Americans give birth to 100 pairs of twins.

64.

Americans give birth to 10,000 new Americans. At least 100 of them are born outside a hospital. The illustration on this page shows the number of babies born in 20 minutes.

65.

Four thousand children and teenagers take up smoking.

10,000

In one day Americans give birth to 10,000 new Americans.

66. Americans receive 5,000 tons of advertising mail. That's enough to heat a quarter million homes. The mountain of mail above weighs 5,000 tons.

IN ONE DAY:

67.

The U.S. Postal Service prints 93 million—more than 22 acres—of postage stamps. It takes 3,200 pounds of flavored glue to stick them all onto envelopes.

68.

Americans find 20 million catalogs in their mailboxes. They return the favor by ordering $123 million of mail-order stuff. On an average day, for example, they order 550 pairs of Maine Hunting Shoes from L. L. Bean, Inc., or about one pair for every 275 L. L. Bean catalogs mailed out. Entrepreneurs in this country know a good thing when they see it—they publish 20 new catalogs every day.

69.

Dogs bite 20 mail carriers. The Postal Service spends $3,500 a day on medical help for its dog-bite victims.

70.

The U.S. Postal Service handles 176 million first-class letters. About 800 of them are reported lost by either the sender or the receiver. It's popular to blame the post office, but based on those figures, a person would have to mail a letter a day for more than 600 years before one would get lost en route. Altogether, the post office handles 345 million pieces of mail a day—enough to fill 2 million bushel baskets.

71.

Twenty thousand people write a letter to the President of the United States.

72.

Americans write half a million letters to Congress.

at trains and another 20 reports of people intentionally leaving things on railroad tracks. There are 2 reports a day of people shooting guns at trains.

75.

22,000 foreigners visit the United States.

76.

Twenty trains accidentally jump their tracks. At least one derailment a day involves hazardous material.

IN ONE DAY:

73.

Trains in this country haul 4 million tons of material in 58,000 railroad cars, equivalent in weight to picking up every person west of the Mississippi, except the Californians, and moving them back east. The 58,000 railroad cars, made into one long train, would stretch 600 miles.

74.

There are 20 reports of people throwing rocks

77.

The hearts of Americans collectively pump out 8 million kilowatt-hours of energy, enough to run 150 throbbing locomotives for 24 hours.

78.

California gains another 1,287 people, the largest population increase of any state.

79.

Five Americans accidentally kill themselves or someone else with a firearm.

80.

Thirty-five Americans die in industrial accidents; another 6,000 suffer disabling injuries.

81.

The U.S. "center of population," an imaginary

point at which the population of this country would balance—north and south, east and west—creeps about 35 feet to the southwest.

82.

Americans lay about 2,750 acres of pavement. That's enough concrete and asphalt to make a bicycle path seven feet wide stretching from the Atlantic to the Pacific coast.

83.

The U.S. Armed Forces lose at least two soldiers to fatal, off-duty motor vehicle accidents.

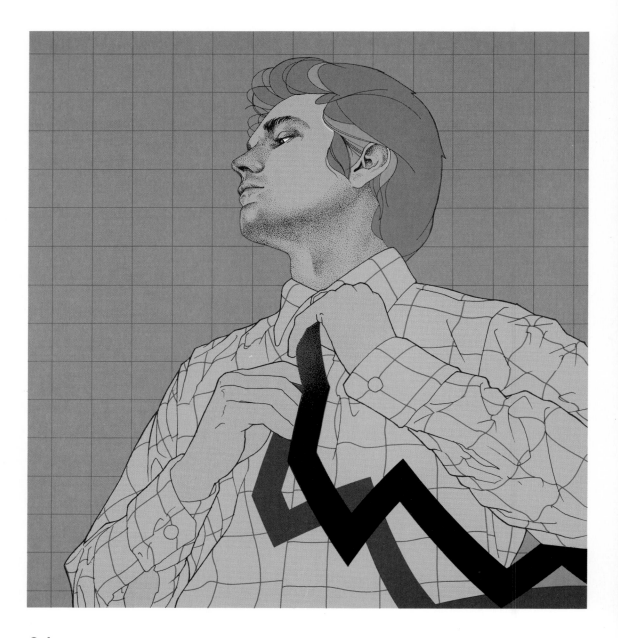

84. Americans buy 200 miles worth of men's neckties—about a quarter of a million ties. Women currently buy 65 percent of all men's ties, down from 85 percent just five years ago.

IN ONE DAY:

85.

Americans spend $300 million on clothes.

86.

Enterprising Americans start 1,700 new corporations.

87.

American marketing experts publish eight or nine new market surveys.

88.

Americans buy 38,000 Ken and Barbie dolls. They also buy 55,000 pieces of Barbie doll clothing, which makes the Mattel Corporation, Barbie's creator, one of the world's leading manufacturers of women's clothing.

89.

At least 300 American women go into business for themselves.

90.

Two or three corporations in this country change their names.

91.

Americans spend $125,000 on tours and merchandise associated with Elvis Presley.

92.

Americans make 100,000 speeches. If they were all waiting their turn at the same soapbox, the speakers would form a line 28 miles long. It would take the last speaker nine hours just to walk to the podium.

93.

Americans smoke more than 86 million packs of cigarettes. If, as one source estimates, smokers shorten their lives by 5.5 minutes per cigarette, Americans collectively give up 18,000 years of living for every day they smoke. They also crush out 85,000 bushels of cigarette butts.

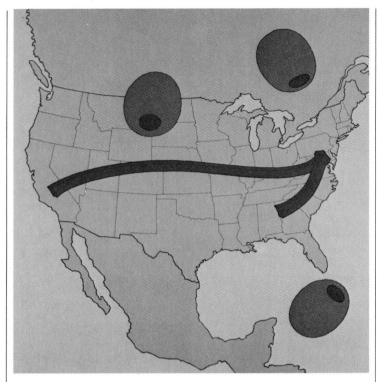

IN ONE DAY:

94.

Americans eat 75,000 pounds of pimento, a small pepper used to make the pimento tape that's stuffed into green olives. That much pimento will make 3,500 miles of pimento tape— enough to stretch from Griffin, Georgia, the pimento capital of the United States, to Lindsay, California, the stuffed-olive capital, via Washington, D.C., the martini capital.

95.

Americans in passenger cars drive 3 billion miles. Imagine a line of cars parked side by side, stretching north to south from Canada to Mexico—1.2 million cars in all. If the whole line of cars were driven straight across the United States from the West Coast to the East, they would have gone collectively about 3 billion miles.

96.

Americans replace 150,000 car batteries. Connected by jumper cables, they would stretch 227 miles.

97.

Americans buy 4 million eraser-tipped wooden pencils. That's enough erasers to remove all the mistakes from 1,500 miles of 8-1/2-by-11 inch notebook paper—about 129 acres of goofs.

98.

Forty Americans fatten their credentials with a phony diploma purchased from a make-believe school or bogus university.

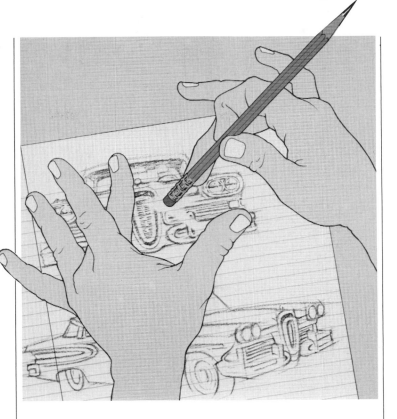

99.

14,000 Americans drop out of, or otherwise give up on, high school.

100.

Americans lose half a million business dollars because of sloppy or illegible handwriting. Luckily, they win an equal amount of money every day in national contests.

101.

Americans buy 426 bushels of paper clips—that's about 35 million clips. According to one estimate, 7 million of them are actually used for clipping paper. Eight or 9 million are lost or swept up with the trash and almost 5 million—that's 61 bushels—are twisted during telephone calls.

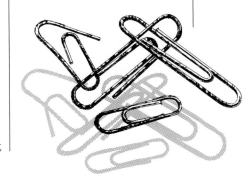

102. U.S. Customs officials seize 1,200 pounds of meat that people try to smuggle into this country.

IN ONE DAY:

103.

McDonald's restaurants serve the equivalent of 2,250 head of cattle to hamburger-hungry customers.

104.

Americans import 575 gallons of drinking water from Mexico.

105.

Americans add 10,000 mink to their closets and coat racks.

106.

Americans bring 2,000 exotic birds into the country that have been captured in the wild. One-fourth of the birds are dead when they arrive, or die before they find an owner.

107.

Americans use 18,000 bushels of tea leaves, enough to make 6 million gallons of tea. The nation's tea bag would fill most of a two-story house.

108.

Spoiled or improperly handled food makes 27,000 Americans sick.

109.

Americans eat a quarter million pounds of lobster, a seafood dinner worth at least $2 million. The national surf-to-turf ratio? One pound of live lobster to 600 pounds of live beef.

110.

Americans eat 18,000 pounds of buffalo meat.

111.

Americans butcher a quarter million hogs, enough to make a line of hogs 165 miles long. Packed together they would cover more than 20 acres. And bacon? Americans eat more than 4 million pounds a day.

IN ONE DAY:

112.

110 lucky golfers make a hole-in-one.

113.

Americans eat 170 million eggs. That's enough unbroken eggs to completely cover a 100-acre golf course. Americans also eat 12 million chickens.

114.

The U.S. Bureau of Engraving and Printing runs off 16 million pieces of paper money, almost half of them $1 bills. That's 41 acres, or seven heaping pickup truckloads of money. All told, there are 9.3 billion bills in circulation—40 apiece for each American. Neatly stacked, they would cover a football field to a depth of eight feet.

115.

Americans buy more than 80,000 pieces of clothing and accessories with little alligators embroidered on them.

116.

Two American public officials are indicted on charges of corruption.

117.

Americans give off enough heat with their bodies to boil 140 million gallons of water. It would take 12 million gallons of gasoline to boil the same amount. The giant percolator in the illustration is the 140-million gallon model. It towers 500 feet above the Rose Bowl stadium.

118.

Americans spend $8 million taking taxis.

119.

Americans use 9.7 million square feet of plate and window glass. That's almost 223 acres of glass, enough to cover 200 football fields.

120.

Americans eat 1.2 million bushels of potatoes. That's a mound of

spuds 230 feet wide and more than 100 feet high.

121.

Americans use 6.8 billion gallons of water to flush their toilets. It would take one gigantic toilet a half mile high— twice the height of the World Trade Center—to

dump that much water in one flush. The Rose Bowl football stadium could fit inside the seat.

122. Americans spend $1 million on rental tuxedos.

IN ONE DAY:

123.

Americans bring 364,000 live wild animals into the country, 337,000 of which are ornamental fish. They also import 296,000 items that are made out of wildlife.

124.

Americans make $350 million under the table from illegal sources—an amount that is never reported to the Internal Revenue Service.

125.

Six million tons of manure hit the ground behind farm animals in this country. That's enough manure to fill a creek 50 feet wide, 10 feet deep, 70 miles long, and too thick to paddle.

126.

Animal shelters in this country destroy 30,000 unwanted cats and dogs.

127.

Ten or eleven Americans receive medical treatment for vitamin overdoses.

128.

Americans dig up $13.7 million to spend on flowers, seeds, and potted plants.

129.

Americans are x-rayed 650,000 times. According to government sources, 250,000 of the x-rays are unnecessary.

130.

Americans make 240,000 pounds of licorice candy. Licorice lovers—there must be some somewhere—eat 1,465 miles of licorice twists every day.

131.

Americans chew up 95 tons of sardines. The gentleman holding his nose in the illustration is examining a freshly opened—95-ton size—can of sardines.

30,000

In one day Americans destroy 30,000 unwanted cats and dogs.

132. Americans weave 640 acres of carpet—that's one square mile. The gentleman in the drawing is using 640 acres of farmland for a carpet; the buildings on his game board are the size of real houses.

IN ONE DAY:

133.

Americans collectively grow six square miles of skin.

134.

Americans add another 150,000 miles of wire to their telephone network.

135.

American miners dig up 2.3 million tons of coal. A day's load of coal would fill 45,000 railroad cars, enough to make a train stretching 475 miles, from central Kentucky to the Atlantic coast. Spilled on the ground, 2.3 million tons of coal would cover a square mile of ground to a depth of three feet. Fifty coal miners are seriously injured on the job every day.

136.

1,100 businesses dissolve or go under. Most do so for voluntary reasons such as the retirement of the owner. About 160 businesses a day go bankrupt.

137.

Americans produce 1.5 billion pounds of hazardous waste. If the problem were shared equally, every adult in the United States would have to find something to do with 9 pounds a day. If they stuffed it in 55-gallon drums, the drums would cover 418 acres.

138.

Miners dig up 625 acres of land in this country—almost one square mile. They clean up and replant about 337 acres a day.

139.

The U.S. Bureau of Engraving and Printing runs 12 million pieces of worn-out money through a paper shredder. That's 400 bushels of bills.

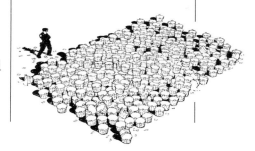

make a pair of synthetic pants with an inseam a mile long. Anyone big enough to wear them would need a belt 300 feet wide and 6,600 feet long to hold them up.

142.

Two hundred Americans have their breasts enlarged, 90 have their breasts reduced, and 35 have their breasts lifted or aimed in some other direction.

IN ONE DAY:

140.

Americans make 5,000 coffins. Most of them are made of sheet metal, 900 are wood that is covered with cloth, 600 are carved out of polished hardwood, 160 are made of copper, bronze or stainless steel, and a few—25—are made of plastic.

141.

Americans weave 1,500 acres of cotton fabric. They also make 2,560 acres, or four square miles, of synthetic fabric. That's enough to

143.

Americans write 100 million checks. A million of them are no good. The good checks would cover a 250-acre field;

the bad checks would cover a 2-1/2-acre trampoline.

144.

Forty Americans injure themselves in trampoline accidents.

145.

More than 100 Americans have a knee replaced.

146.

Americans change 60 million diapers, most of them on children less than two years old. Forty-eight million diapers are thrown out after one use.

147.

Sixty Americans are murdered. More than

half are shot, 12 are stabbed, 4 or 5 are strangled, and at least 2 fall victim to a blunt object.

148.

Americans eat more than 400,000 bushels of bananas, the country's most popular fruit. America's daily banana would measure 192 feet long and 43 feet in diameter.

149.

Thirty-five Americans fall to their deaths.

BONUS FACT

▶ IN ONE DAY more than 90,000 Americans are injured by consumer products. Following are some of the products and the numbers of people who require emergency room treatment every day:

Stairs, steps, and ramps	2,100
Bicycles and accessories	1,420
Chairs, sofas, beds, and mattresses	1,200
Nails, carpet tacks, screws, and thumbtacks	690
Bottles, jars, cans, and other containers	640
Drinking glasses	300
Clothing, shoes, and accessories	250
Hammers	150
Carpets and rugs	140
Pencils, pens, and other desk supplies	120
Bricks and concrete blocks	120
Needles and pins	110
Toilets and sinks	90
Television sets	75
Trash cans and waste containers	60
Home decorations and artificial plants	40
Paper bags and wrappers	35
Ice picks and skewers	30
Beach chairs and folding chairs	20
Blenders, mixers, and food processors	20
Tool boxes	20
Ash trays	15
Nonelectric musical instruments	15
Aquariums and accessories	15

150. Americans eat 6.5 million gallons of popcorn. Seventy percent of it is eaten at home. The giant clown above is relaxing on a 6.5-million-gallon pile of popcorn.

IN ONE DAY:

151.

Americans still buy more than a million boxes of Cracker Jacks.

152.

Half a million Americans visit an amusement park; 33 come away with injuries.

153.

Americans spend $200 million on advertising, enough to paper 77,000 billboards with one-dollar bills.

154.

Americans print 62.5 million newspapers on 23,000 tons of newsprint. That's 164 square miles of paper, enough to line a bird cage 12 miles wide and 13 miles long.

155.

Americans eat 400,000 gallons of canned corn. That's equal to one huge can, 57 feet tall and 37 feet in diameter.

156.

Thirty Americans celebrate their 100th birthday. About 5,500 Americans (their children?) turn 65.

157.

Americans snort a bathtub full of cocaine—325 pounds in all. Every day, 5,000 people try the drug for the first time.

158.

Americans drink 3 million gallons of orange juice. That's enough to fill a glass 110 feet tall and 70 feet in diameter.

159.

There are more than 50 symphony orchestra performances in this country. Sixty thousand people attend.

160.

Cartoonists submit more than 300 cartoons to the New Yorker magazine.

in this country are making 25 trillion decisions each second, or more than 100,000 decisions a second for each American.

164.

Americans give away $165 million, or nearly $2,000 a second.

165.

Three Americans are accidentally electrocuted.

166.

Americans use 72 million pounds of wheat flour. Baked into bread, it would make a loaf the length of a football field, 175 feet wide and more than 200 feet high. The flour itself, spilled down

IN ONE DAY:

161.

Two hundred Americans become millionaires.

162.

Dishonest employees cost American businesses close to $30 million, about the cost of giving every employee in this country an annual bonus of $100.

163.

The average American's name crops up in a computer somewhere 35 times. As you read these words, computers

a mountainside, would make a ski slope 300 feet wide, 14 inches deep, and more than a mile long.

167.

126 Americans lose their eyesight. On the brighter side, 2,000 Americans a day have some of their vision restored through surgery.

168.

Americans gnaw on 90,000 bushels of fresh carrots. That's equal to one 2,300-ton carrot, 26 feet wide at the top and 179 feet long.

169.

The United States gains more than 5,000 people (the result of births and immigration minus deaths and emigration). There are 5,000 dots in the illustration.

170.

Americans swipe 100,000 doses of narcotics, stimulants, and depressants from pharmacies, drug manufacturers, hospitals, and doctors' offices.

171.

Americans fork out $14.3 million for lottery tickets.

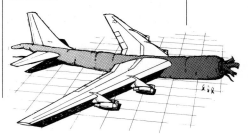

172. The U.S. Geological Survey prepares—for the first time—detailed topographical maps for about 100 square miles of the United States. Some eastern states, low in mineral resources, have hardly been mapped at all.

IN ONE DAY:

173.

Water washes 11 million tons, or about 8.8 million cubic yards, of topsoil from this country. It would take a line of heavy trucks 3,500 miles long to haul that much topsoil.

174.

Manufacturers in this country pass out 392 million coupons with a total face value of more than $70 million. That's 11 million square feet of coupons, enough to cover 250 acres. Less than 4 percent of the coupons are ever redeemed. That's about 10 acres. To top it off, manufacturers lose $220,000 a day because of fraudulent or poorly managed coupon redemptions.

175.

Americans throw out 150,000 tons of boxes, bags, and wrappers. It would take 10,000 tractor-trailer trucks to haul that much junk to the dump—a line of trucks more than 120 miles long. Some people avoid the dumps altogether. Every day, they sprinkle a million bushels of litter out the windows of their cars and trucks.

176.

Americans buy 275,000 pounds of yarn. That's enough to knit sweaters for everyone in Anchorage, Alaska—175,000 people.

177.

Americans saw up and pound together 100 million board feet of wood. That's enough to make a wooden nickel 39 feet thick and 523 feet in diameter. Flooring mills alone turn out 15 acres of hardwood floor, enough to make a nice plaque for the wooden nickel.

arrested for arson. The human toll? Eighteen Americans a day are killed in fires and more than 80 are seriously injured. Five or six people die every day in fires caused by untended cigarettes.

180.

Americans jack up 225 full-size houses, load them onto trucks, and haul them to new locations.

181.

Americans nail down 400 acres of asphalt roofing.

182.

Americans make 1.9 million sheets of plywood. That's more than

IN ONE DAY:

178.

Americans slap on 3 million gallons of paint and other brush-on coatings, enough to repaint the White House 10,000 times (any color you like). Three million gallons of paint would spruce up 200,000 average-size houses.

179.

There are 7,000 fires reported in this country, 2,750 of them in buildings. Of those, 350 are intentionally set or are of suspicious origin. Fifty people a day are

two square miles of laminated wood. Placed end to end, the sheets would easily reach from one side of the United States to the other.

183.

Students physically assault more than 200 teachers. They also beat up 12,000 other students.

184.

100,000 Americans move to a different home. Eighteen thousand move to a different state.

185.

Americans eat 1.7 million pounds of canned tuna—enough to make 15.7 million tuna-salad sandwiches. The tuna alone would make a cube measuring 20 feet on a side; the sandwiches, spread on the ground, would cover 50 acres.

186.

Americans finish building 3,000 new single-family houses. They also finish 650 new mobile homes, more than 60 percent of which end up parked in the southeastern states.

187.

Americans process more than 100,000 bushels of shelled or roasted peanuts. Imagine a mound of peanuts 100 feet wide and 48 feet high. Almost one-third of the pile is blended into a quarter-million gallons of peanut butter, enough to make a gooey glob the size of a two-story house. The odd-looking house in the illustration is fashioned from a day's worth of peanut butter.

188.

Six thousand Americans buy houses that someone else has already lived in.

189. Americans eat more than 200 million pounds of fresh fruit and vegetables—enough to fill 4,000 railroad cars.

IN ONE DAY:

190.

Americans eat 815 billion calories of food—roughly 200 billion more than they need to maintain a moderate level of activity. That's enough extra calories to feed everyone in Mexico, a country of 80 million people.

191.

Ten Americans die from accidental poisoning.

192.

Americans produce 50 gallons of mercury. That's enough to fill a bathtub eight or nine inches deep. A bathtub full of mercury weighs 5,650 pounds—14 times the weight of a bathtub full of water.

193.

Americans produce 4 million pounds of pesticide; 2.7 million pounds a day is spread on this country.

194.

Americans hand over $40 million to prostitutes.

195.

Americans buy 4,100 Official Swiss Army knives, and countless imitations which no doubt end up a disappointment to their owners.

196.

Americans find something to do with a million bushels of tomatoes. A million-bushel basket would stand 100 feet high and measure 150 feet across the top.

197.

Americans use 11,000 tons, or 550,000 bushels, of apples. About half of them are eaten fresh, presumably putting millions of doctors out of work. America's daily pile of apples would be 180 feet wide and 80 feet high.

gold. That's enough to cast a 16-foot cube of lead, a 23-foot cube of copper, and a 27-inch cube of silver. One day's cube of gold, worth twice as much as the 16-foot block of lead, would measure less than 7-1/2 inches.

IN ONE DAY:

198.

Twenty banks are robbed. Average take: about $2,500.

199.

Americans buy 65,000 hand-held calculators. At this rate, it would take almost ten years to buy one calculator for every person in the country.

200.

Americans dig up and refine 1,500 tons of lead, 3,400 tons of copper, 7,560 pounds of silver, and 272 pounds of

201.

Twenty-five children are injured by coins.

202.

150 law enforcement officers are physically assaulted.

203.

Americans toss 70 million quarters into arcade game machines—

enough quarters to completely cover ten football fields.

204.

Americans feed vending machines more than 250 million coins worth $34 million. Piled together the coins would total 8,680 cubic feet, a volume illustrated by the giant piggy bank on this page.

205.

Americans inject themselves with 25 pounds of heroin.

206.

Americans earn $123 million selling illegal drugs. That's more money than 5,000 narcotics officers earn in a year.

207.

The U.S. Mint stamps out 3.5 million quarters, 3.7 million dimes, 3 million nickels, and 39 million pennies. That's 300 heaping wheelbarrows full of coins. The pennies alone would fill 210 wheelbarrows or most of a 10-foot cube.

208. Americans spend $55 million for auto repairs that are unnecessary, faulty, or downright fraudulent. That's enough money to buy 500,000 bicycles a day, or more than enough to buy one bicycle a year for everyone old enough to ride a bike.

IN ONE DAY:

209.

Thirteen hundred cars and trucks catch on fire. Two people are killed; ten are seriously injured.

210.

Americans purchase 25,000 new automobiles. At least a fourth of them are made outside the United States.

211.

Americans smash up 50,000 cars and trucks. Five thousand people are injured and more than 120 are killed. Twenty-five Americans die every day who would have been saved by air bags that inflate upon impact. They also would have been saved by seatbelts, but only one in ten Americans uses them.

212.

137,000 Americans stay home from work because they have a cold. 164,000 children stay home from school with the same excuse.

213.

Eighteen hundred Americans have their bicycles swiped.

214.

The population of Detroit, Michigan, drops by another 79 people, more than any other city in the United States. Michigan itself loses more people than any other state—165 a day.

215.

Americans see at least three UFOs that are convincing enough to report to the authorities.

216.

Americans pucker up to 23,500 bushels of fresh lemons. The lemon on this page is a one-day supply—52 feet long and 33 feet high.

50,000

In one day Americans smash up 50,000 cars and trucks.

217. Americans manufacture enough artificial Christmas trees to artificially reforest eight acres of land. The giant in the drawing is napping in the middle of an eight-acre woods. The handle of his axe is almost 300 feet long.

IN ONE DAY:

218.

The mannequin population in this country increases by more than 250. That's almost 100,000 plastic people a year, enough to pack the largest sports arena.

219.

Americans drift off to sleep with the help of six heaping pickup truckloads of sleeping pills—30 million tablets in all.

220.

Americans quarry 2 million tons of sand and gravel, enough to make a driveway 1,000 miles long. Imagine a monstrous pile of sand and gravel 600 feet wide and 380 feet high. Americans also dig up 122,000 tons of clay and 2,000 tons of peat every day.

221.

175 Americans injure themselves with chain saws.

222.

Americans chop down 1,000 trees and string them up as telephone poles.

223.

Five thousand ducks and other waterfowl die from accidentally eating lead shotgun pellets that have fallen in the shallow water where they feed. Each winter, hunters deposit another 6,000 tons of shot.

224.

Americans make 25 acres of artificial turf, enough to carpet 9,000 patios.

225.

Americans smoke 85,000 pounds of marijuana. That's a bale of pot the size of a small house. This easygoing fellow is relaxing on a day's worth of dope.

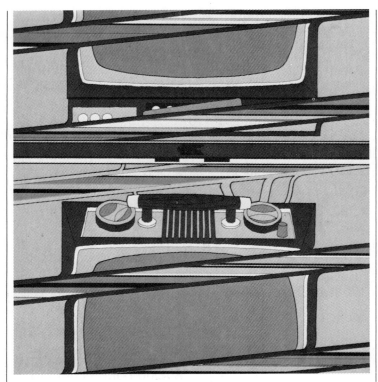

fancier, warm up 2 million pounds of frozen entrees and "nationality" dishes.

228.

Americans toss out 20,000 TV sets. That's a pile of sets 80 feet in diameter and almost 50 feet high.

229.

Americans stamp out 574,000 record albums and 342,000 singles; they import another 66,000 records of one type or another. Playing them all would take 50

IN ONE DAY:

226.

The average American is exposed to 1,600 commercial messages by one medium or another. Of these, 80 are noticed, and only 12 elicit some kind of response—usually negative. The average child watches more than 50 television commercials a day.

227.

Americans eat 1.3 million TV dinners, the kind with a tray and several compartments. Other people, looking for something a little

years. Every day Americans copy 1.3 million record albums on tape. That costs record stores about $8 million in lost sales.

230.

18,000 household burglaries are reported in the United States, an average of 13 every minute. Half the time, burglars enter a house without having to break a lock or window.

231.

Americans install 8,000 feet—more than a mile and a half—of chain-link fence.

232.

One million Americans visit museums. Most Americans would rather

visit a science museum than a history museum. But more of them would rather visit a history museum than an art museum.

233.

Americans spend $11 million to have their radios and televisions fixed. That means that,

all over the country, radios and televisions are blinking out to the tune of $7,650 a minute.

234.

Thieves steal 35 art objects from museums, galleries, churches, private homes, and archeological sites—a daily take worth $137,000.

235. Americans fill in, or at least try to fill in, about 50 acres of crossword puzzles. The gentleman in the illustration is taking a crossword break on a 50-acre puzzle.

IN ONE DAY:

236.

Americans patch up 50 miles of road and 10 or 11 bridges.

237.

Americans have to deal with parking almost 110 million cars. If every car owner in the United States were to visit Rhode Island at the same time, they would completely blanket the state with their parked cars.

238.

Americans pump 82 billion gallons of water out of the ground, 10 billion for use in private homes. Every day they drill a thousand new water wells.

239.

Americans skin 98,200 cattle, 8,300 calves, and 17,700 lambs and sheep. In all, the animals give up more than 4 million square feet of hide, enough to cover 92 acres.

240.

Americans drop $5.5 million into parking meters. Even so, they shell out three times that much in parking meter fines. The U.S. parking meter population hovers around one million; 140 meters a day are replaced because they are worn out or broken; 6 or 7 a day are cracked open or stolen.

241.

2,200 Americans discover that they have cancer; about 1,000 a day die from the disease.

242.

Americans eat 2.8 million pounds of fresh cucumbers. That's equal to a cucumber 100 feet long and 28 feet thick.

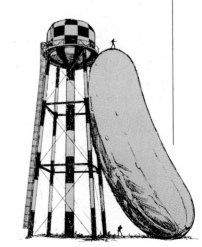

of blue cheese, 700,000 pounds of cream cheese, 650,000 pounds of Swiss, and 5.8 million pounds of cheddar. Cottage cheese alone makes up more than 2.5 million pounds, or 312,000 gallons, of the daily diet. The drawing on this page shows part of the country's daily cheese plate.

IN ONE DAY:

243.

Dairy cows in this country produce 47 million gallons of milk—enough to fill a milk carton 360 feet tall. Only 19 million gallons are used as liquid milk. The rest is used to make cheese, yogurt, and other dairy products.

244.

Americans wiggle into 25,000 new leotards.

245.

Americans eat 12.5 million pounds of cheese, including 85,000 pounds

246.

Americans eat 1.5 million pounds of lard—imagine a tub of lard 50 feet in diameter and 13

feet deep. That's enough lard to make a 90-acre pie crust.

247.

American rats and mice do damage to buildings and crops totaling $2.5 million. And before the rats and mice get to the crops, American farmers lose a third to insects, disease, and weeds.

248.

Students in public schools throw out $3 million worth of lunch food.

249.

Americans send 9 million greeting cards, almost half of them for birthdays. That's more than 6 birthday cards apiece—how many did you get on your birthday? Every year, Americans mail out 2.7 billion Christmas cards (12 apiece), and 900 million Valentines (4 apiece).

250.

City trucks haul half a million tons of municipal garbage to the dump.

251.

Americans snap up 82,000 mousetraps.

252.

Americans eat 3 million gallons of ice cream and ice milk. Imagine three scoops of ice cream, any flavor you like, that are each 65 feet in diameter.

253.

1,250 Americans have their tonsils taken out. Another 850 lose their appendixes.

254.

Americans eat 3 million pounds of butter and 7 million pounds of margarine. The drawing on this page shows a day's supply of each.

255. Almost 140,000 Americans commute to work across the United States border, leaving the country—at least temporarily—10,000 tons lighter.

IN ONE DAY:

256.

The United States expels 2,300 illegal aliens. About 50 of them are physically removed from the country; the rest are, in official lingo, "required to depart."

257.

Americans collectively pass more than 9 million cubic feet of gas. That's enough to inflate a balloon 250 feet in diameter.

258.

For civilian use alone, American gunsmiths make 6,700 pistols and revolvers, 4,000 rifles, 2,500 shotguns, and depending on demand, from 50 to 200 machine guns. Thieves in this country steal 275 guns a day from law-abiding owners.

259.

Americans mix 187,000 tons of Portland cement, enough to make a concrete sidewalk four feet wide, winding 3,000 miles—from Portland, Maine, to Portland, Oregon.

260.

Americans buy 3.6 million incandescent light bulbs, enough to completely cover three acres of ground. Even with the sockets right in front of them, it would take two people a year, working 12-hour shifts, to replace that many light bulbs.

261.

Americans use 57 billion kilowatt-hours of energy. That's equal to burning 1.6 billion gallons of gasoline. If each person in the country simultaneously touched off 422 pounds of TNT, they'd release about the same amount of energy.

patients don't pull through. All told, 67,000 people a day meet with the business end of a surgeon's knife.

265.

Seven thousand hospital patients become infected with an illness other than the one that sent them to the hospital.

266.

4,100 Americans are circumcised. As a result, 200 of them suffer what surgeons call "excessive penile loss."

IN ONE DAY:

262.

Eighty Americans die from adverse reactions to prescription drugs.

263.

100,000 Americans are admitted to the hospital for one reason or another—that's roughly the population of Ann Arbor, Michigan. The average stay is just over a week.

264.

Americans undergo 5,000 unnecessary surgical operations. Twenty-five of the

267.

Americans perform 500 coronary bypass operations, making it the most common major operation performed in this country.

268.

Two million Americans visit a doctor's office. Waiting in line, single file, 2 million patients would stretch 750 miles.

269.

American hospitals serve 7 million meals. Even so, 135 hospital patients die every day from what one study called inadequate nutritional care.

270.

Americans spend $800 million on personal health care. That's $3.50 per person per day spent on everything from hospital care to drugs and eyeglasses.

271.

Americans spend $12,000 on dental floss.

272.

2,700 Americans discover that they have gonorrhea. Two hundred discover that they have syphilis.

273.

Americans receive 6 million telephone calls from someone trying to sell them something. Assuming no one calls at an unreasonable hour, that's 8,000 people a minute who answer the phone—only to hear a sales pitch.

274.

Americans swallow 52 million aspirin tablets. That's more than 575 bushels of pain reliever. The gentleman in the illustration is standing next to a day's worth of pills.

275.

American researchers need 135 new monkeys and apes for their experiments.

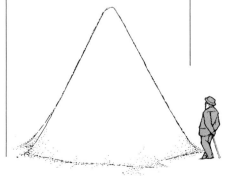

276. Americans drink 23 million gallons of soft drinks, enough to fill a soda bottle 530 feet tall.

IN ONE DAY:

277.

Americans eat 50 million pounds of sugar. That's 833,000 cubic feet of sugar a day or an average of 21 teaspoons apiece for everyone in the country.

278.

Americans spend $300 million eating out. The national daily bar tab—drinks and tips—is $64 million.

279.

Americans wrest 18 million tons of raw material from its natural state. If all Americans shared the job equally, they would each have to dig up, saw down, or gather more than 150 pounds of stuff every day.

280.

Americans use 126 million glass bottles and jars. If the glass containers used in one day were placed side by side along the centerline of a highway, they would easily reach from one coast of the United States to the other.

281.

Americans buy 2,500 new motorcycles, partly because they smash up 1,500 a day in accidents.

282.

Americans use a quarter million tons of steel, enough to forge a solid steel spike the size of the Washington Monument.

283.

Smugglers fly 150 plane-loads of illegal drugs into the country. That's one shipment every ten minutes.

284.

Americans knit 9.3 million pairs of socks. The enormous laundry bag in the illustration contains a day's worth of new socks.

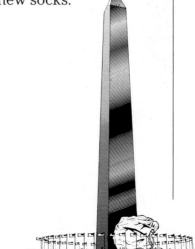

1,650 stars—about 3 hours and 20 minutes worth of bites.

288.

Americans spend $3.6 million on toys and accessories for their pets. They spend $27,000 a day on pet clothing alone. Each winter, pet owners in this country buy more than 400,000 T-shirts for their dogs.

IN ONE DAY:

285.

Americans buy ten tons of colored aquarium gravel.

286.

Dogs and cats in this country give birth to 70,000 new dogs and cats. That's 500 bushel baskets full of squirming puppies and kittens.

287.

Dogs bite 12,000 Americans. Sixty of the victims need a plastic surgeon to patch them up. The pattern behind the man in the drawing has

289.

During winter months, Americans feed wild birds $1 million worth of bird food.

290.

Americans feed their dogs more than 10,000

tons of dog food. The tiny people in the illustration are standing next to 10,000 tons, or 663,000 cubic feet, of dry dog food.

291.

Americans give 4,125 gallons of blood, enough to completely drain and refill 2,000 people.

292.

Americans pump 365 million gallons of crude oil out of the ground

and import another 147 million gallons from other countries. The total is more than half a billion gallons or nine quarts apiece for each American. That's enough to fill an oil can 550 feet tall and 400 feet in diameter.

293.

Eighteen cases of rabies are reported in animals. Human rabies is limited to one or two cases a year.

294.

There are three incidents involving a bomb. Thieves in this country make off with 127,000 pounds of explosives and 150,000 feet of fuse

and detonator cord each year. Fortunately, most of it is recovered unused.

295.

Americans buy at least 5 million things that are shaped like Mickey Mouse, or have a picture of Mickey Mouse on them.

296.

Americans spend $25 million getting their kids to and from school.

297. Americans discover at least one new species of insect.

IN ONE DAY:

298.

At least 50 electronic bugging devices are secretly installed by Americans who, for one reason or another, want to spy on someone else.

299.

The Smithsonian Institution adds 2,700 things to its collections.

300.

100,000 cattle are herded into slaughter-houses. That's a line of animals 135 miles long. They leave as 60 million pounds of meat, enough to make a steak ten feet thick and big enough to cover the playing field in Yankee Stadium.

301.

Americans stitch together 833,000 pairs of jeans—590,000 for men, and 243,000 for women. Stacked in a pile, the jeans made in a day would measure twice the size of a two-story, four-bedroom house.

302.

Four people in this country discover that they have malaria.

303.

Americans use more than 40 acres of leather, most of it to cover their feet. Almost a million people, the population of, say, Dallas, could stand on a 40-acre piece of leather and never get their boots dirty.

304.

Nine hundred Americans claim to have used a firearm to protect themselves or thwart a robbery.

305.

Americans treat themselves to 56,000 gallons of honey. That's enough honey to fill seven tractor-trailer tank trucks.

80

100,000

In one day Americans herd 100,000 cattle into slaughterhouses.

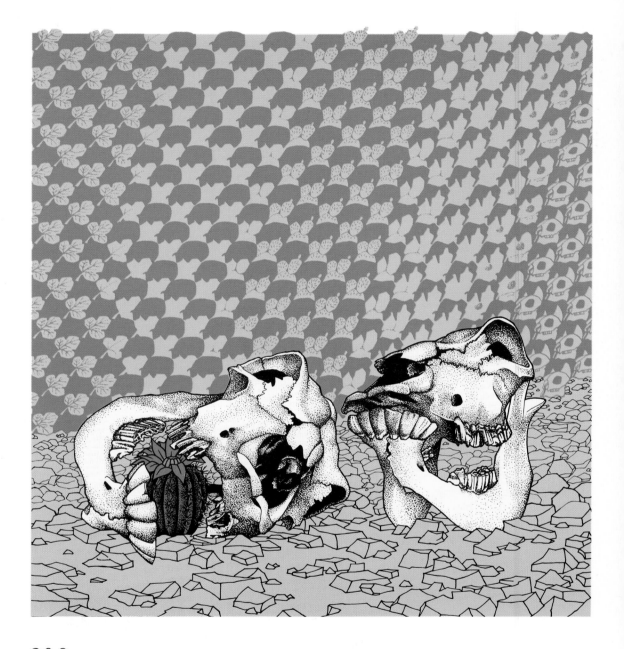

306. Americans use 150 billion gallons of water for irrigation. That's enough water to fill a jug a half mile wide and three times the height of the Empire State Building.

IN ONE DAY:

307.

Americans import the skins of 12,000 reptiles along with 400 lizard-skin watchbands and 20,000 other items made from the hides of lizards and snakes. They also find some reason to import the skins of 400 ostriches, 350 kangaroos, and more than 100 frogs and toads.

308.

Two hundred dogs are poisoned by pesticides. Fifty of them die. Pesticides kill 30 cats, 25 cattle, 10 horses, and about 6,000 fish every day. They also poison 125 people, 8 of whom require admission to a hospital.

309.

Americans produce 88 million gallons of moisture by breathing and perspiring.

310.

Americans drain, fill, or pave over 1,100 acres of swamp and wetland.

311.

Americans produce three more tons of radioactive waste.

312.

Americans need 115 million gallons of drinking water to quench their thirst. Imagine a tumbler of ice water, 500 feet tall and 200 feet in diameter.

313.

Americans buy 8,000 wild cacti that were dug up in some other country.

314.

Americans drink 1.5 million gallons of wine, enough to fill a wine bottle 190 feet tall and 50 feet wide at its base.

take three and a half hours to walk from one end to the other.

318.

Americans import 3,000 ivory carvings and knickknacks. That's enough ivory to make perfectly good tusks for 20 elephants.

319.

Six hundred Americans try to kill themselves and more than 70 of them succeed. Of those, more than 40, mostly men, use firearms. Fifteen Americans end

IN ONE DAY:

315.

Americans treat themselves to 5,000 tons of candy.

316.

Dentists put more than 80 pounds of gold in

Americans' mouths. All told, they fill half a million cavities a day.

317.

Americans buy 12,000 new refrigerators and 10,000 new kitchen ranges. That's a line of appliances more than 11 miles long—it would

their lives with poison, 10 hang or strangle themselves, and 6 or 7 use other methods, including explosives.

320.

800,000 Americans take off in a passenger plane.

321.

More than 5,000 Americans jump out of airplanes. Almost all of them wear parachutes.

322.

American dentists see one million patients. That's 12 times the crowd at the Sugar Bowl.

323.

Americans scrub their teeth with 550,000

pounds of toothpaste. That's almost 2.5 million tubes of dentifrice. The giant tube in the drawing holds 550,000 pounds of toothpaste.

324.

Americans snap 21 million photographs. That's more than 29 acres of wallet-size photos. Working ten hours a day, it would take two years to flip through them all.

325. Americans eat 8,500 tons of fresh lettuce. Measuring 90 feet in diameter, an 8,500-ton head of iceberg lettuce would in fact make a pretty respectable iceberg.

IN ONE DAY:

326.

1,750 people immigrate to the United States and 430 become U.S. citizens. About 12 people a day have their petitions for citizenship denied.

327.

Americans cook 247,000 pounds of fish sticks. Imagine one monstrous sandwich with a fish stick the size of a large house trailer.

328.

Americans add another 85 cubic feet of books, films, documents, and letters to their National Archives for permanent storage. That's about six steamer trunks of stuff added to the nation's attic.

329.

Fifty-five Americans die who qualify as organ donors. Seven of them actually donate their organs, which are transplanted into 14 or 15 other people.

330.

Americans make 800 million telephone calls; that's more than 15 centuries of one-minute conversations. America's daily long distance phone bill is $120.6 million, or almost $84,000 a minute. Every day, Americans make $300,000 worth of long distance calls that they never pay for.

331.

The federal government issues another 100 pages of rules and regulations.

332.

Americans take 100,000 bushels of broccoli to market. About half of it is eaten fresh. The two stately stalks on this page represent a day's broccoli. They each tower 84 feet; their trunks are more than 10 feet thick.

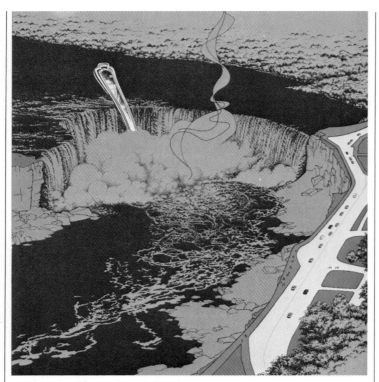

would take a full 30 seconds for 17 million gallons of it to flow over the Horseshoe Falls.

335.

Americans pass 88 million gallons of urine. It would take more than 2.5 minutes for that much liquid, let's call it water, to flow over the Horseshoe Falls.

336.

Homeowners in this country spend $6 million fixing their plumbing. They spend almost $9 million patching their roofs.

337.

Americans drink 2.75 million gallons of bottled water, almost half

IN ONE DAY:

333.

Americans buy 35,000 new coffeemakers. That's more than 30 million watts of coffee brewing machinery. If everyone ran home from the store and plugged in a new coffeemaker at the same time, together they would draw the same electric power as ten speeding subway trains.

334.

Americans drink 17 million gallons of coffee. Imagine the Niagara River filled with steaming black coffee; it

of it in California. The average wholesale price per gallon is $1.35—somewhat higher than the average price of gasoline.

338.

Seventeen Americans drown.

339.

Americans lose one million gallons of gasoline to evaporation at gas stations and other gasoline fueling facilities. The glass jug in the illustration holds a million gallons of gas, enough to fuel the average car for 2,000 years.

340.

Americans drink 1.2 million gallons of hard liquor. That's enough

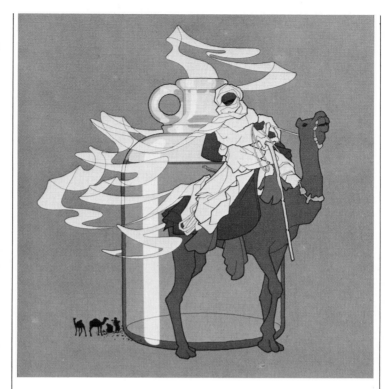

booze to get 26 million people thoroughly stewed.

341.

Americans have to cut and stack 115,000 cords of firewood to keep their woodsheds full. It would take ten people, working eight-hour days, more than 31

years to cut and stack that much wood. Their woodpile would make a 245-foot cube.

342. Americans use 187,000 tons of paper. Made into newsprint, that much paper would cover 1,350 square miles, an area the size of Long Island.

IN ONE DAY:

343.

The U.S. Border Patrol catches 2,250 people who are sneaking into the country, out of the country, or smuggling something across the border. They question 39,000 people a day.

344.

Americans, and extremely resourceful ones at that, export 6,000 tons of used paper in exchange for money.

345.

Americans launch 1,500 new boats. They already have 13 million, enough to completely encircle the lower 48 states with a ring of boats. In fact, you would have to squeeze the boats in sideways to make them fit.

346.

The U.S. Coast Guard rescues 16 people.

347.

The fishing industry in this country processes 33 million pounds of fish and shellfish. Two-thirds of the seafood, or 22 million pounds, is used for human food; a million pounds is fed to animals. The rest is used to make chemicals and paint.

348.

Americans gobble up 75 acres of pizza. Imagine 13 pizzas the size of the Roman Colosseum—that's enough food to cover 60 football fields.

349.

Americans eat 88,000 bushels of green peppers. That's 352,000 pecks of peppers, enough to make a pile 100 feet wide and 42 feet high.

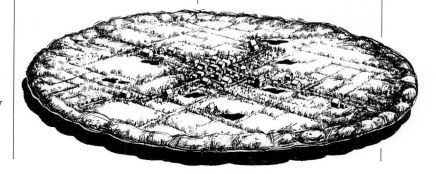

length of a ten-mile race course. Altogether, Americans buy 2.3 million pairs of shoes a day, enough to line the bottom of a 17-acre closet. More than half of the shoes are imported.

352.

The hearts of Americans collectively pump more than 400 billion gallons of blood, equal to the flow of the Mississippi River at Vicksburg.

IN ONE DAY:

350.

Americans need 3.4 billion cubic feet of oxygen to keep from smothering. That's a cube of oxygen measuring 1,500 feet on a side. To get that much oxygen, Americans need to process 67 billion cubic feet of air with their lungs. That's a cube of air measuring 4,000 feet on a side.

351.

Americans buy 52,000 pairs of running shoes. The empty boxes alone would stretch the

353.

5,500 Americans embark on a cruise.

354.

827,000 American adults need some sort of help getting out of bed. About one million need help going to the toilet, and almost three million depend on someone else to help them walk around.

355.

Americans fork over $3 million for bridge, ferry, tunnel, and highway tolls.

356.

Americans eat 5.8 million pounds of chocolate candy, enough to make a candy bar the size of a football field and two feet thick. The Hershey Chocolate Company alone, running full blast, can churn out a quarter million pounds of Hershey's Kisses. That's

enough to fill the beds, and collapse the springs, of 55 pickup trucks.

357.

Americans jog 28 million miles—enough to travel every road in the United States seven times over. While running, they burn off 2.8 billion calories. That's roughly the number of calories in one million pounds of milk chocolate. The statue above is made with a million pounds of chocolate.

IN ONE DAY:

358.

137,000 bolts of lightning strike the United States. Lightning kills 125 people outright each year and injures 500 others. Sound dangerous? Kiddie rides at amusement parks injure just as many people.

359.

Americans build five new nuclear weapons.

360.

175 Americans, aged 65 and older, get married—8 of them for the first time. Others, 13,500 a day, can't wait that long and marry at a younger age. More than 6,500 Americans a day get divorced.

361.

Americans watch 1.5 billion hours of television. That's equal to 2,300 human lifetimes spent in front of the tube every day.

362.

Three Americans change their sex from man to woman, or woman to man.

363.

More than 8,000 Americans become pregnant by mistake.

364.

5,500 Americans die for one reason or another. Lying side by side in a field of daisies, they would take up an acre of space. Standing in line at the Pearly Gates, they would stretch for a mile and a half.

365.

One thousand pounds of extraterrestrial material reaches the surface of the United States. Most of it is cosmic dust that enters the atmosphere and sifts slowly to earth. Smaller than the dust in a sunbeam, about one particle lands per square yard every day.

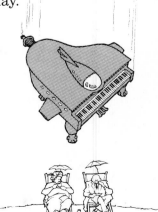